Saturation

Aeron P. White

For my parents, who have struggled, persevered, and achieved more than 50 years of marriage.

For my son, Brandon and my daughter, Rebecca, may their future be bright and their hardships few.

CONTENTS

ACKNOWLEDGMENTS

Thanks to ChatGPT3.5 for valuable research material.

Thanks to OpenArt.ai for the illustration support.

1 FOREWORD

In a world inundated with information, choices, and expectations, the saturation of society has become a defining characteristic of contemporary life. From the constant barrage of digital content to the relentless pursuit of material possessions, the effects of saturation permeate every aspect of our existence. Yet, amidst this abundance, questions arise: What drives this saturation? How does it impact our psychology, our communities, and our planet? And most importantly, what can we do to stop it and shape a future where saturation no longer reigns supreme?

In "Saturation," we embark on a journey of exploration into the depths of human behaviour, societal dynamics, and the intricate interplay between psychology and culture. Drawing upon research, interdisciplinary perspectives, and real-world examples, this book delves into the psychology of social norms and expectations, uncovering the mechanisms that drive conformity, influence, and change within society.

From the roots of social norms and the psychology behind their formation to the far-reaching effects of saturation on individual well-being, social cohesion, and environmental sustainability, each chapter offers a nuanced examination of the complex forces at play in our modern world. We explore the cultural, economic, and technological drivers of saturation, shedding light on the underlying causes that have propelled society to its current state of abundance and excess.

But this book is not merely an exposé of the problems we face; it is a call to action—a manifesto for change. Through thoughtful analysis and practical insights, we chart a path forward towards stopping the saturation of society and envisioning a future where sustainability, equity, and well-being take centre stage. From promoting mindful consumption and fostering resilient communities to advocating for policy reform and embracing technological innovation responsibly, we explore the myriad ways in which individuals, communities, and institutions can come together to shape a more sustainable and fulfilling future for humanity.

As we unravel the tapestry of social norms and expectations woven throughout society, we are reminded of the power we hold—to challenge the status quo, to redefine cultural norms, and to shape the course of history. In the pages that follow, may you find inspiration, empowerment, and a renewed sense of purpose as we embark on this collective journey of transformation. Together, let us unravel the tapestry of saturation and weave a brighter, more sustainable future for generations to come.

Welcome to "Saturation". The journey begins here...

2 UNDERSTANDING THE PSYCHOLOGY OF SOCIAL NORMS AND EXPECTATIONS

Human behaviour is heavily influenced by social norms and expectations, which are unwritten rules and standards of behaviour that guide individuals' actions within a society or group. Social norms shape our beliefs, attitudes, and behaviours by providing a framework for understanding what is considered acceptable or appropriate in a given context. Understanding the psychology behind social norms and expectations can help elucidate why individuals conform to these standards and the impact they have on individual and collective behaviour.

Social identity theory posits that individuals derive a sense of self-concept and self-esteem from their membership in social groups. People tend to categorize themselves and others into ingroups (groups to which they belong) and outgroups (groups to which they do not belong). In order to maintain a positive social identity and sense of belonging, individuals conform to the norms and expectations of their ingroup, aligning their behaviour with the group's values and standards.

Normative social influence refers to the tendency for individuals to conform to social norms in order to gain approval, acceptance, or avoid disapproval or rejection from others. This form of social influence is driven by the desire to fit in and be liked by others, rather than a genuine belief in the correctness or validity of the norm. Individuals may conform to social expectations even when they privately disagree with them in order to avoid social sanctions or ostracism from their peers. Informational social influence occurs when individuals conform to social norms because they believe that others possess superior knowledge or expertise about the situation. When faced with uncertainty or ambiguity, people look to others for guidance on how to behave, particularly in novel or unfamiliar situations. By conforming to the behaviour of others, individuals can gain valuable information about what is considered appropriate or acceptable in a given context. Cognitive dissonance theory suggests that individuals experience psychological discomfort when their beliefs, attitudes, or behaviours are inconsistent with one another. In order to reduce this discomfort, people may adjust their attitudes or behaviours to align with social norms and expectations, even if it means compromising their own values or preferences. Conforming to social norms can help individuals maintain internal consistency and reduce cognitive dissonance by bringing their beliefs and actions into harmony with one another.

From an evolutionary perspective, conformity

to social norms and expectations may have served adaptive functions in promoting survival and group cohesion. Throughout human history, conformity to group norms may have facilitated cooperation, coordination, and collective action, thereby increasing the likelihood of survival and reproduction. As such, individuals may be predisposed to follow social norms and expectations as a means of enhancing their social status, acceptance, and inclusion within the group. Cultural factors also play a significant role in shaping social norms and expectations, as they vary across different societies and cultural contexts. Cultural norms dictate appropriate behaviours, values, and beliefs within a given society, influencing how individuals interact with one another and navigate social situations. Socialization processes, cultural traditions, and institutional practices transmit these norms from one generation to the next, shaping individuals' understanding of their roles and responsibilities within society.

The psychology of humans following social norms and social expectations is complex and multifaceted, influenced by factors such as social identity, normative and informational social influence, cognitive dissonance, evolutionary psychology, and cultural influences. Understanding these psychological mechanisms can provide insights into why individuals conform to social norms and expectations and the impact they have on individual and collective behaviour within society.

3 THE SATURATION OF SOCIAL MEDIA

"A Landscape of Less Meaningful Content"
Social media, once hailed as the harbinger of a new era of connectivity and meaningful interaction, has become inundated with a deluge of less meaningful content. This phenomenon stems from various interconnected factors, reflecting the evolution of technology, human behaviour, and the dynamics of online communities.

In the quest for likes, shares, and followers, many users and content creators have succumbed to the allure of quantity over quality. The pressure to maintain a consistent online presence has led to a proliferation of hastily produced, low-effort content. Memes, viral challenges, and clickbait headlines reign supreme, often overshadowing content that fosters genuine engagement and critical discourse. Social media platforms, driven by algorithms designed to maximize user engagement and advertising revenue, often prioritize content that elicits immediate reactions. These algorithms reward sensationalism, polarization, and superficiality, effectively amplifying the spread of less meaningful content while relegating more nuanced and substantive posts to the sidelines.

In an era characterized by instant gratification, attention spans have dwindled, and the demand for bite-sized, easily digestible content has surged. Quick-fix entertainment, such as short videos, memes, and listicles, dominates social media feeds, catering to users' desire for immediate stimulation rather than deeper exploration or reflection.

The rise of influencer culture has further fuelled the proliferation of less meaningful content on social media. Influencers, motivated by the pursuit of fame, fortune, and brand partnerships, often prioritize self-promotion and curated lifestyles over authentic expression or substantive discourse. This quest for validation through likes and followers perpetuates a cycle of superficiality and shallowness. Social media algorithms, designed to personalize users' experiences based on their preferences and browsing history, inadvertently contribute to the formation of echo chambers and filter bubbles. Users are exposed primarily to content that aligns with their existing beliefs and interests, reinforcing biases and limiting exposure to diverse perspectives and meaningful discourse. In the attention economy, where users' attention is a finite and valuable resource, social media platforms compete fiercely for engagement. This relentless pursuit of user attention incentivizes the production and promotion of content optimized for virality and shareability, often at the expense of depth, authenticity, and meaning.

The saturation of social media with less meaningful content can have profound psychological effects on users. Constant exposure to curated, highlight-reel versions of others' lives can foster feelings of inadequacy, comparison, and FOMO (fear of missing out). Moreover, the dopamine-driven feedback loop of likes, comments, and shares can fuel addictive behaviours and detract from real-world relationships and experiences. The saturation of social media with less meaningful content reflects a complex interplay of technological, societal, and psychological factors. While social media undoubtedly offers opportunities for connection, creativity, and expression, its current landscape underscores the need for greater awareness, critical engagement, and perhaps a re-evaluation of our online habits and priorities. As users, content creators, and platform developers, we must strive to cultivate spaces that prioritize authenticity, empathy, and genuine human connection amidst the noise and superficiality of the digital realm.

4 THE SATURATION OF THE NEWS AND PRESS

In recent years, the news and press landscape has undergone a profound transformation characterized by an unprecedented abundance of information, platforms, and voices. This saturation of the news and press has reshaped the way we consume and interact with media, presenting both opportunities and challenges for individuals, society, and democracy.

One of the primary drivers of saturation in the news and press is the proliferation of news sources, both traditional and digital. With the advent of the internet and social media, anyone with an internet connection can become a publisher or content creator, leading to a vast array of news outlets, blogs, podcasts, and citizen journalism platforms. This proliferation of sources has democratized access to information but has also led to fragmentation, polarization, and the spread of misinformation. The rise of the 24/7 news cycle has contributed to the saturation of the news and press by creating a constant demand for new content and updates. News organizations and digital platforms compete for audience attention in an increasingly crowded marketplace, leading to sensationalism, clickbait, and the prioritization of speed over accuracy.

This relentless news cycle can overwhelm audiences with a constant stream of information and contribute to information fatigue and disengagement.

The blurring of lines between news and entertainment has contributed to the saturation of the news and press. Many news outlets prioritize sensationalism, celebrity gossip, and human-interest stories over in-depth reporting and investigative journalism. This focus on entertainment value and audience engagement can distort the public discourse, trivialize important issues, and undermine the credibility of the news media. Social media platforms have emerged as influential players in the news and press landscape, amplifying the saturation of information and contributing to filter bubbles and echo chambers, as mentioned in the previous chapter of this book. Algorithmic news feeds prioritize content based on users' past behaviour and preferences, reinforcing existing beliefs and perspectives and limiting exposure to diverse viewpoints. This can contribute to polarization, misinformation, and the spread of fake news within online communities. The commercialization and corporate ownership of news media have also contributed to the saturation of the news and press. Many news outlets are owned by large conglomerates with vested interests in advertising revenue and audience engagement. This can lead to conflicts of interest, biased reporting, and the prioritization of profit over journalistic integrity. Moreover, the decline of traditional advertising revenue models has led to the rise of native advertising, sponsored content, and clickbait headlines, further blurring the line between editorial content and advertising. The saturation of the news and press is exacerbated by information overload and the attention economy, where news organizations and digital platforms compete for audience attention in a crowded marketplace. This can lead to the prioritization of sensationalist headlines, viral content, and emotionally charged stories that capture audience attention and drive clicks. Moreover, the constant bombardment of news alerts, notifications, and updates can overwhelm audiences and contribute to information fatigue and burnout.

The saturation of the news and press is driven by a combination of factors, including the proliferation of news sources, the 24/7 news cycle, infotainment and sensationalism, social media, commercialization and corporate ownership, and information overload. Identifying and addressing the root causes of saturation requires systemic changes, shifts in media practices, and media literacy education to empower individuals to navigate the complexities of the modern news landscape and make informed decisions about the information they consume. In a later chapter of this book we will explore the root causes of saturation in more detail.

5 THE SATURATION OF CONSUMERISM

"A Phenomenon of Excess and Consequence" Consumerism, the relentless pursuit of material goods and the belief in their ability to bring happiness and fulfilment, has permeated every facet of modern society. From the relentless bombardment of advertisements to the proliferation of disposable products, the current landscape is characterized by a saturation of consumerist ideals. This phenomenon is shaped by a multitude of factors, including economic systems, cultural norms, and technological advancements, each contributing to a cycle of excess and consequence. At the heart of consumerism lies the omnipresent influence of advertising and marketing. Brands spend billions of dollars each year crafting meticulously targeted campaigns designed to stimulate desire and create a sense of inadequacy that can only be remedied through consumption. From billboards and television commercials to sponsored social media posts, consumers are bombarded with messages that equate happiness, success, and identity with material possessions.

In the pursuit of perpetual growth and profit, planned obsolescence has become a pervasive strategy employed by manufacturers across industries. Products are intentionally designed to have a limited lifespan or become outdated quickly, prompting consumers to replace them with newer models or versions. This cycle of built-in obsolescence not only drives consumption but also contributes to environmental degradation and resource depletion. The rise of disposable culture epitomizes the excesses of consumerism. Single-use products, from plastic water bottles to fast fashion garments, are mass-produced and quickly discarded, contributing to overflowing landfills and pollution of the natural environment. The convenience and affordability of disposable goods have fostered a throwaway mentality that prioritizes convenience over sustainability and longevity.

Consumerism is often fuelled by the desire for status and social validation. The acquisition of luxury goods, designer labels, and conspicuous displays of wealth serve as symbols of success and social standing. In a culture that equates material possessions with personal worth, individuals may engage in excessive consumption to signal their affluence and belonging within their social circles. The advent of e-commerce and digital marketplaces has revolutionized the landscape of consumerism. Online shopping platforms offer unprecedented convenience and accessibility, allowing consumers to browse and purchase goods with the click of a button. However, the digital realm also amplifies the pressures of consumerism through targeted advertisements, personalized recommendations, and social comparison, perpetuating a cycle of constant consumption. Consumerism is deeply intertwined with the economic systems that prioritize endless growth and consumption as drivers of prosperity. Capitalist economies rely on consumer spending to fuel economic growth and maintain market stability. As a result, individuals are encouraged to participate in the endless cycle of production and consumption, perpetuating a culture of materialism and excess. The saturation of consumerism can have profound psychological effects on individuals and society as a whole. The relentless pursuit of material possessions and status can lead to feelings of emptiness, anxiety, and dissatisfaction, as the fulfilment promised by consumerist ideals remains elusive. Moreover, the constant cycle of acquisition and disposal can contribute to a sense of environmental despair and disconnection from the natural world.

The saturation of consumerism represents a complex interplay of economic, cultural, and psychological factors that shape modern society. While consumption is an inherent part of human existence, the current landscape underscores the need for greater awareness, mindfulness, and ethical consumption practices. As consumers, we must critically examine our values and priorities, challenging the notion that happiness and fulfilment can be found through the endless acquisition of material possessions. By fostering a culture of sustainability, conscious consumption, and meaningful connection, we can begin to counteract the detrimental effects of consumerism and create a more balanced and harmonious relationship with the world around us.

6 THE SATURATION OF THE JOB MARKET

In the landscape of modern employment, the job market and career pathways have become increasingly saturated, presenting both challenges and opportunities for individuals seeking to establish themselves professionally. This saturation is influenced by a multitude of factors, including economic trends, technological advancements, demographic shifts, and evolving labour market dynamics.

The saturation of the job market is shaped by broader economic realities, including fluctuations in economic growth, globalization, and industry-specific trends. In periods of economic downturn, job opportunities may become scarcer as companies tighten their budgets and prioritize cost-cutting measures. Conversely, during periods of economic expansion, the job market may appear more robust, but competition for desirable positions remains fierce. Technological advancements, such as automation, artificial intelligence, and digitalization, have reshaped the job market and disrupted traditional career pathways. Certain industries and occupations have experienced significant upheaval as tasks previously performed by humans are automated or outsourced to machines. As a result, workers must adapt to changing skill requirements and embrace lifelong learning to remain competitive in a rapidly evolving labour market. The saturation of the job market is exacerbated by a persistent skills mismatch, where the skills possessed by job seekers do not align with the demands of employers. Rapid technological innovation and evolving industry trends necessitate a constant upskilling and reskilling of the workforce. However, many individuals struggle to acquire the necessary skills or access relevant training opportunities, leading to a disconnect between supply and demand in the labour market. The rise of the gig economy and non-traditional forms of employment has contributed to the saturation of the job market and the proliferation of precarious work arrangements. Freelancing, temporary contracts, and on-demand labour platforms offer flexibility and autonomy to workers but often lack the stability, benefits, and job security associated with traditional employment.

As a result, many individuals navigate a patchwork of gigs and side hustles in pursuit of financial stability and career advancement.

The saturation of the job market is further intensified by global competition, as advancements in communication and transportation facilitate the outsourcing of jobs to low-cost labour markets overseas. Additionally, skilled workers from around the world compete for employment opportunities in increasingly interconnected and borderless industries. This globalization of the labour market presents challenges for domestic job seekers but also creates opportunities for cross-cultural collaboration and international career mobility. Demographic shifts, such as population growth, generational changes, and aging workforces, influence the saturation of the job market and career trajectories. Millennials and Generation Z enter the workforce with different values, expectations, and career aspirations than previous generations, challenging traditional notions of work-life balance, job security, and loyalty to employers. Moreover, an aging population and prolonged workforce participation among older adults can lead to increased competition for jobs and limited advancement opportunities for younger generations. Amidst the saturation of the job market, entrepreneurship and innovation emerge as pathways for individuals to carve out their own career opportunities and pursue their passions. The democratization of technology and access to resources has empowered aspiring entrepreneurs to launch startups, small businesses, and social enterprises. Entrepreneurial endeavours offer autonomy, creativity, and the potential for financial success but also entail risks, uncertainties, and the need for resilience in the face of failure.

In surviving the saturation of the job market and careers, individuals must adopt a proactive and adaptable mindset, embracing lifelong learning, skill development, and entrepreneurial thinking. Strategies such as networking, mentorship, and professional development can help individuals differentiate themselves in a competitive job market and seize emerging opportunities. Furthermore, policymakers, educators, and employers play crucial roles in addressing systemic challenges and fostering an inclusive, resilient, and dynamic labour market that supports the diverse aspirations and talents of the workforce.

7 THE SATURATION OF MODERN LIFE

"Balancing Priorities in an Age of Abundance" In the contemporary landscape, characterized by constant connectivity, information overload, and a culture of productivity, people's lives have become increasingly saturated with commitments, responsibilities, and stimuli. This saturation extends beyond mere busyness; it encompasses the relentless pursuit of achievement, consumption, and fulfilment within finite lifetimes. Navigating this saturation requires individuals to strike a delicate balance between competing priorities, cultivate mindfulness, and reevaluate their relationship with time and purpose.

The proliferation of digital technologies has transformed nearly every aspect of daily life, blurring the boundaries between work, leisure, and personal time. Smartphones, social media, and ubiquitous connectivity ensure that individuals are constantly bombarded with notifications, emails, and demands for attention. This digital overload not only contributes to feelings of overwhelm and distraction but also impedes the ability to disconnect and recharge, leading to burnout and mental fatigue.

In a society that glorifies productivity and busyness as markers of success and worth, individuals often feel pressure to maximize every moment and optimize their lives for efficiency. The pursuit of productivity can lead to a relentless cycle of workaholism, self-improvement endeavours, and the constant quest for optimization in all areas of life. However, this obsession with productivity can come at the expense of creativity, spontaneity, and genuine relaxation. The abundance of choices available in modern life can paradoxically lead to decision paralysis and analysis paralysis. Whether it's selecting a career path, choosing from an array of consumer products, or deciding how to allocate leisure time, individuals may feel overwhelmed by the myriad options available to them. This abundance of choice can lead to indecision, anxiety, and a sense of dissatisfaction, as individuals second-guess their decisions in search of the elusive "best" option. The prevalence of social media exacerbates feelings of saturation by fostering a culture of comparison and FOMO (fear of missing out). Scrolling through curated feeds filled with highlight reels of others' lives can breed feelings of inadequacy, envy, and the constant need to keep up with perceived societal norms and expectations. The pressure to showcase one's achievements, experiences, and possessions on social media fuels a cycle of consumption and comparison, perpetuating feelings of saturation and dissatisfaction.

Despite technological advancements that

promise to save time and increase efficiency, paradoxically, many individuals experience a pervasive sense of time scarcity. The demands of work, family responsibilities, social obligations, and personal pursuits often exceed the available hours in a day, leading to feelings of stress, exhaustion, and a perpetual sense of being "behind" schedule. The elusive quest for work-life balance becomes increasingly challenging in a world where time is perceived as a finite and scarce resource. In navigating the saturation of modern life and the finite nature of time, individuals must prioritize self-awareness, intentionality, and self-care. Cultivating mindfulness practices, such as meditation, journaling, or spending time in nature, can help individuals reclaim a sense of presence and perspective amidst the noise and busyness of daily life. Moreover, setting boundaries, practicing saying no, and delegating tasks can empower individuals to reclaim control over their time and energy, allowing for a more balanced and fulfilling existence. Ultimately, navigating the saturation of modern life requires a willingness to reassess priorities, embrace imperfection, and cultivate a sense of gratitude for the richness and complexity of the human experience, even within the constraints of finite lifetimes.

8 THE SATURATION OF POLITICS

"Navigating a Global Landscape of Polarization and Complexity"

In today's interconnected world, politics has permeated nearly every aspect of public discourse, shaping individual beliefs, societal values, and international relations. The saturation of politics is evident in the proliferation of news coverage, social media debates, and grassroots activism that touch on a wide range of issues, from governance and policymaking to social justice and human rights. This phenomenon reflects the increasing complexity, polarization, and significance of political dynamics on both local and global scales. The digital age has ushered in an era of information overload, where individuals are inundated with news, opinions, and commentary from a multitude of sources. As mentioned in the previous two chapters of this book, social media platforms, 24-hour news networks, and online forums provide constant updates and analysis on political developments, often blurring the lines between journalism, advocacy, and misinformation. This flood of information can be overwhelming, making it difficult for individuals to discern fact from fiction and navigate the complexities of political issues.

Politics has become increasingly polarized, with ideological divides deepening and tribalism on the rise. Partisan loyalty often takes precedence over compromise and collaboration, leading to gridlock and dysfunction within political institutions. The rise of echo chambers and filter bubbles further exacerbates polarization, as individuals gravitate towards news sources and social circles that reinforce their existing beliefs and values. This tribalistic mindset hinders constructive dialogue and inhibits the search for common ground on pressing issues. The saturation of politics is amplified by globalization and interconnectedness, which have blurred the boundaries between domestic and international affairs. Economic integration, migration flows, and transnational threats such as climate change and terrorism require coordinated responses and cooperation among nations. Political decisions made in one country can have far-reaching implications for others, underscoring the interconnected nature of contemporary politics and the need for multilateral engagement and diplomacy. Many individuals harbour a deep sense of disillusionment and distrust towards traditional political institutions, such as governments, political parties, and elected officials. Scandals, corruption, and perceived ineffectiveness erode public confidence in the ability of these institutions to address pressing challenges and represent the interests of ordinary citizens. This disillusionment has fuelled populist movements and anti-establishment sentiment, challenging the legitimacy of established political elites and traditional modes of governance.

Identity politics has emerged as a dominant force in contemporary political discourse, with issues of race, gender, ethnicity, religion, and sexuality playing a central role in shaping political identities and agendas. Identity-based movements advocate for the recognition of marginalized groups, the redress of historical injustices, and the promotion of diversity and inclusion in political decision-making. However, identity politics can also exacerbate divisions and tensions within society, as competing groups vie for power and recognition. Despite the challenges posed by political saturation, activism and grassroots mobilization have flourished as individuals seek to effect change and hold their governments accountable.

Social movements, protests, and advocacy campaigns galvanize public support and pressure policymakers to address systemic injustices and inequalities. The digital realm provides a platform for organizing and mobilizing across geographic boundaries, empowering citizens to amplify their voices and demand political reform.

In overcoming the saturation of politics worldwide, individuals must strive for informed citizenship, critical thinking, and civic engagement. Seeking out diverse perspectives, fact-checking information, and engaging in respectful dialogue with those who hold differing views are essential steps towards fostering a more inclusive and deliberative political discourse. Moreover, holding elected officials accountable, participating in democratic processes, and advocating for systemic reforms are integral to shaping a political landscape that reflects the values of transparency, accountability, and social justice. While the saturation of politics presents challenges, it also offers opportunities for collective action and solidarity in pursuit of a more equitable and democratic future.

9 THE SATURATION OF ROADS

"Challenges and Solutions in the Western World"
In the Western world, the saturation of roads has become a pervasive and pressing issue, characterized by congested highways, urban gridlock, and strained transportation infrastructure. This phenomenon is influenced by a combination of factors, including population growth, urbanization, economic development, and changing mobility patterns. As cities and regions grapple with the consequences of road saturation, policymakers, urban planners, and transportation authorities are tasked with finding sustainable solutions to alleviate congestion, improve mobility, and enhance the quality of life for residents. Population growth and urbanization are

significant drivers of road saturation in the Western world. Rapid urban expansion, coupled with demographic shifts towards urban areas, has led to increased demand for transportation services and infrastructure. As cities become more densely populated, road networks face greater pressure to accommodate growing volumes of vehicular traffic, exacerbating congestion and travel delays.

The prevalence of car dependency in the Western world contributes to road saturation, as personal vehicles remain the primary mode of transportation for many individuals and households. Reliance on cars for daily commuting, errands, and leisure activities places strain on road networks, particularly during peak travel times. Moreover, the proliferation of single-occupancy vehicles contributes to inefficiencies in road usage and exacerbates congestion.

Inadequate public transit systems exacerbate road saturation by limiting viable alternatives to private car travel. Many cities in the Western world face challenges related to underfunded or outdated public transit infrastructure, insufficient service coverage, and unreliable schedules. As a result, individuals may opt for personal vehicles out of necessity or convenience, further congesting roads and contributing to environmental pollution. Infrastructure deficiencies, including outdated roadways, inadequate signage, and insufficient capacity, contribute to road saturation and exacerbate congestion. Aging infrastructure may struggle to accommodate modern traffic volumes and vehicle types, leading to bottlenecks, accidents, and delays. Furthermore, insufficient investment in road maintenance and expansion hampers efforts to address growing transportation demand and improve road safety.

The saturation of roads in the Western world has significant environmental implications, including air and noise pollution, habitat fragmentation, and greenhouse gas emissions. Increased vehicular traffic contributes to urban air pollution and respiratory health problems, while the expansion of road networks can encroach upon natural habitats and disrupt ecosystems. Additionally, reliance on fossil fuel-powered vehicles exacerbates climate change, highlighting the need for sustainable transportation solutions. Technological innovations and mobility solutions offer promising avenues for addressing road saturation in the Western world. Advancements in intelligent transportation systems, including traffic management technologies, real-time data analytics, and smart infrastructure, enable more efficient use of existing road networks and improved traffic flow. Furthermore, the emergence of shared mobility services, electric vehicles, and micro-mobility options presents opportunities to reduce car dependency, alleviate congestion, and mitigate environmental impacts.

Addressing road saturation requires integrated planning and policy solutions that prioritize sustainable transportation modes, land use planning, and multi-modal connectivity.

Governments, urban planners, and transportation authorities must collaborate to develop comprehensive strategies that promote public transit expansion, active transportation infrastructure, and demand management measures. Additionally, investment in alternative transportation modes, such as cycling infrastructure, pedestrian-friendly streetscapes, and transit-oriented development, can help reduce reliance on cars and create more liveable, resilient communities.

With the saturation of roads in the Western world, stakeholders must embrace a holistic approach that balances the need for efficient mobility with environmental sustainability, equity, and quality of life considerations. By prioritizing investments in public transit, active transportation, and innovative mobility solutions, communities can create more resilient, inclusive, and vibrant urban environments that enhance mobility options for all residents while mitigating the adverse impacts of road saturation.

10 THE SATURATION OF THE CAR INDUSTRY

The car industry, once synonymous with freedom, mobility, and innovation, has reached a state of saturation in many parts of the world. This saturation is characterized by a multitude of factors that have reshaped the landscape of the automotive sector, from the proliferation of car models to changing consumer preferences and emerging technological advancements. Understanding the root causes and effects of saturation in the car industry is essential for navigating its complexities and shaping its future trajectory.

One of the primary drivers of saturation in the car industry is the proliferation of car models offered by manufacturers. With the globalization of supply chains and the advent of advanced manufacturing technologies, automakers can produce a wide array of vehicles to cater to diverse consumer preferences and market segments. This proliferation has led to a crowded marketplace with numerous options for consumers, ranging from compact cars to SUVs, electric vehicles (EVs), and luxury sedans.

The saturation of the car industry is further exacerbated by market fragmentation and intense competition among manufacturers. Globalization and free trade agreements have opened up new markets and increased competition, leading to price wars, aggressive marketing tactics, and constant product innovation. This has created a highly competitive environment where automakers vie for market share, driving down profit margins and increasing pressure to innovate and differentiate their products.

Shifting consumer preferences and lifestyle trends have also contributed to the saturation of the car industry. Millennials and younger generations are increasingly gravitating towards urban living, shared mobility solutions, and alternative transportation modes such as ride-hailing, car-sharing, and public transit. Moreover, growing awareness of environmental issues and sustainability concerns has led to increased demand for electric and hybrid vehicles, further diversifying the automotive market.

Technological advancements, particularly in the fields of electric vehicles, autonomous driving, and connectivity, are reshaping the future of the car industry and driving saturation in new directions. The rise of electric vehicles (EVs) and battery technology is disrupting traditional combustion engine vehicles and prompting automakers to invest heavily in electrification and sustainable mobility solutions. Likewise, the development of autonomous driving technology and in-vehicle connectivity is transforming the driving experience and opening up new opportunities for innovation and growth.

Market saturation and oversupply are significant challenges facing the car industry, particularly in mature markets such as North America and Europe. With a limited pool of potential buyers and increasing competition, automakers are forced to offer aggressive incentives, discounts, and lease deals to stimulate demand and clear excess inventory. This can lead to pricing pressures, margin erosion, and an unsustainable business model in the long run.

Environmental regulations and sustainability concerns are also driving saturation in the car industry by shaping consumer preferences and influencing product development. Governments around the world are implementing stricter emissions standards and incentivizing the adoption of electric and zero-emission vehicles to reduce greenhouse gas emissions and combat climate change. This has prompted automakers to invest in electric and hybrid technology and transition towards more sustainable mobility solutions.

The saturation of the car industry is driven by a combination of factors, including the proliferation of car models, market fragmentation and competition, changing consumer preferences, technological advancements, market saturation and oversupply, and environmental regulations and sustainability concerns. Navigating the complexities of saturation in the car industry requires strategic planning, innovation, and adaptation to emerging trends and market dynamics. Through understanding the root causes and effects of saturation, car manufacturers can position themselves for success in an increasingly competitive and dynamic marketplace whilst maintaining a focus on sustainability.

11 THE SATURATION OF PUBLIC TRANSPORT

"Challenges and Strategies"

Public transport plays a critical role in providing mobility, accessibility, and sustainability in urban areas worldwide. However, the saturation of public transport systems presents significant challenges, including overcrowding, service unreliability, and infrastructure strain. Understanding the complexities of public transport saturation is essential for developing effective strategies to improve service quality, expand capacity, and enhance the overall passenger experience.

Rapid urbanization and population growth have placed unprecedented demands on public transport systems in cities around the world. As urban populations swell and cities expand, the need for efficient, reliable, and accessible transportation options becomes increasingly critical. However, many public transport networks struggle to keep pace with growing demand, leading to overcrowded trains, buses, and stations during peak travel times. The saturation of public transport systems is often exacerbated by capacity constraints, where infrastructure and vehicles operate at or near maximum capacity.

Limited investment in expanding and

modernizing public transport infrastructure, including tracks, stations, and rolling stock, hampers efforts to accommodate growing ridership and improve service reliability. As a result, passengers may experience delays, overcrowding, and reduced comfort during their journeys. Public transport saturation can disproportionately affect marginalized communities and low-income individuals who rely heavily on public transit for their daily mobility needs. Service gaps, inadequate coverage, and affordability barriers may restrict access to essential services, employment opportunities, and educational institutions for vulnerable populations. Addressing equity and accessibility concerns requires targeted interventions, such as fare subsidies, paratransit services, and infrastructure improvements in underserved areas.

Improving the efficiency and effectiveness of public transport systems requires greater integration and inter-modality with other modes of transportation, such as cycling, walking, and ride-sharing. Seamless connections between different transit services, as well as with first- and last-mile mobility options, enhance the overall passenger experience and encourage modal shift away from private car usage. Furthermore, integrated fare systems, real-time information, and multimodal trip planning tools facilitate more convenient and user-friendly travel experiences. Advancements in technology, such as intelligent transportation systems, digital ticketing, and real-time passenger information, offer opportunities to optimize public transport operations and improve service quality. Predictive analytics, machine learning, and automated scheduling can help transit agencies anticipate demand, optimize routes, and mitigate disruptions more effectively. Additionally, electrification, automation, and zero-emission technologies contribute to reducing the environmental impact of public transport systems and enhancing sustainability. Addressing the saturation of public transport requires strategic policy interventions and sustained investment in infrastructure, operations, and maintenance. Governments and transit agencies must prioritize public transport as a cornerstone of sustainable urban development and allocate sufficient funding to support its expansion and improvement. Moreover, regulatory reforms, public-private partnerships, and innovative financing mechanisms can unlock additional resources and expertise to enhance the resilience and performance of public transport systems. To Navigate through the saturation of public transport, stakeholders must adopt a collaborative and multi-faceted approach that combines infrastructure investment, policy reform, technological innovation, and community engagement.

By prioritizing equity, accessibility, and sustainability, cities can develop public transport systems that meet the diverse needs of their residents, reduce congestion, and enhance overall quality of life. Moreover, fostering a culture of public transport usage through education, outreach, and promotional campaigns can encourage modal shift and create a more inclusive and sustainable urban mobility ecosystem.

12 THE SATURATION OF THE ART AND FINE ART SECTORS

"Trends, Challenges, and Opportunities"
In the contemporary landscape of the art world, saturation has become a prevailing characteristic, marked by an abundance of artists, artworks, galleries, and exhibitions vying for attention and recognition. This saturation is shaped by a multitude of factors, including globalization, technological advancements, shifting cultural norms, and evolving market dynamics. As artists, collectors, and industry professionals navigate this saturated environment, they encounter both challenges and opportunities in their pursuit of creative expression, artistic excellence, and commercial success. The globalization of the art market, facilitated by digital technologies and online

platforms, has democratized access to art and expanded the reach of artists and galleries across geographic boundaries. While this globalization has opened up new opportunities for exposure and collaboration, it has also intensified competition and commodification within the art world. Artists must contend with a crowded marketplace where visibility and relevance are increasingly tied to digital presence, social media engagement, and online sales.

The democratization of art production and distribution has led to a proliferation of artists and artworks in diverse styles, mediums, and genres.

This abundance of creative output contributes to a sense of saturation within the art world, as galleries, museums, and art fairs are inundated with submissions and proposals from emerging and established artists alike. Navigating this competitive landscape requires artists to distinguish themselves through originality, authenticity, and artistic innovation. The art market has become increasingly commercialized, with speculation, investment, and profit-seeking driving transactions and valuations. High-profile auctions, art fairs, and gallery exhibitions often prioritize marketability and investment potential over artistic merit, leading to the commodification of art and the prioritization of certain styles or movements over others. This focus on commercial success can marginalize artists whose work does not conform to prevailing market trends or aesthetic preferences. While saturation presents challenges, it also fosters opportunities for greater accessibility and inclusivity within the art world. Emerging artists, marginalized voices, and underrepresented communities have found platforms to share their stories, perspectives, and experiences through art. Grassroots initiatives, community-based art projects, and online galleries provide spaces for diverse voices to be heard and celebrated, challenging traditional hierarchies and gatekeeping in the art world.

The saturation of the art world has prompted the emergence of new models of exhibition and distribution that challenge conventional norms and structures. Pop-up galleries, artist-run spaces, online marketplaces, and decentralized platforms offer alternative avenues for artists to showcase their work and connect with audiences directly. These innovative models prioritize flexibility, autonomy, and grassroots engagement, empowering artists to retain greater control over their creative practice and professional trajectory. The saturation of the art and fine art sectors, means that artists, collectors, and industry professionals must embrace adaptability, resilience, and creativity. Artists should focus on cultivating their unique voice, honing their craft, and fostering authentic connections with audiences and patrons. Collectors and patrons, in turn, can support emerging talent, champion diversity and inclusion, and prioritize art that resonates on a personal and emotional level. Furthermore, institutions, galleries, and policymakers play a crucial role in fostering an environment that supports artistic experimentation, cultural diversity, and equitable access to the arts. Through embracing innovation and a commitment to artistic excellence, the art world can navigate the challenges of saturation while harnessing its transformative potential to enrich lives and inspire social change.

13 THE SATURATION OF HUMAN POPULATION

"Challenges and Implications"
The human population of the Earth has reached unprecedented levels, with over 7.8 billion people inhabiting our planet as of the latest estimates. This population saturation presents a myriad of challenges and implications, ranging from resource depletion and environmental degradation to social inequality and geopolitical tensions. Understanding and addressing the complexities of population saturation is crucial for ensuring the sustainability and well-being of current and future generations. The human population has experienced exponential growth over the past century, fuelled by factors such as advancements in healthcare, sanitation, and agricultural productivity. While population

growth rates have slowed in some regions, particularly in high-income countries, many developing nations continue to experience rapid demographic expansion. This population growth places strain on natural resources, infrastructure, and social services, exacerbating existing challenges related to poverty, food security, and access to healthcare.

The saturation of the human population has profound implications for the environment, including habitat loss, deforestation, species extinction, and climate change. Increased demand for land, water, and energy resources leads to environmental degradation and ecosystem destruction, threatening biodiversity and ecological resilience. Moreover, the carbon footprint associated with human activities, including industrialization, transportation, and agriculture, contributes to greenhouse gas emissions and global warming, exacerbating environmental crises such as extreme weather events, rising sea levels, and loss of biodiversity. Population saturation intensifies competition for finite resources, including freshwater, arable land, minerals, and fossil fuels. As the global population continues to grow, demands for food, water, and energy escalate, placing pressure on natural ecosystems and depleting non-renewable resources. In regions already experiencing resource scarcity and environmental degradation, population saturation exacerbates existing vulnerabilities and challenges related to access to clean water, adequate nutrition, and sustainable livelihoods. Rapid population growth and urbanization have led to the proliferation of megacities and urban sprawl, placing strain on infrastructure, housing, transportation, and public services. Overcrowded cities face challenges related to congestion, pollution, inadequate housing, and social inequality, exacerbating urban poverty and social exclusion. Moreover, inadequate urban planning and infrastructure development contribute to environmental degradation and public health risks, further compromising the quality of life for urban residents. Population saturation has social and economic implications, including poverty, unemployment, inequality, and social unrest. In regions with high population density and limited resources, individuals may struggle to access basic necessities such as food, shelter, and healthcare, leading to socioeconomic disparities and marginalization. Moreover, population pressure can strain social cohesion and exacerbate tensions related to ethnic, religious, or cultural differences, fuelling conflicts and instability in fragile regions.

Addressing the challenges of population saturation requires a comprehensive approach that integrates social, economic, and environmental considerations. The United Nations Sustainable Development Goals (SDGs) provide a framework for addressing population-related issues, including access to education, healthcare, family planning services, and reproductive rights. By promoting gender equality, empowering women and girls, and investing in education and healthcare infrastructure, countries can achieve demographic transition and promote sustainable development that benefits both people and the planet.

In viewing the saturation of the human population, it is imperative to adopt strategies that promote sustainable consumption, equitable development, and environmental stewardship. This includes investing in education, healthcare, and family planning services, promoting renewable energy and resource-efficient technologies, and fostering international cooperation and solidarity. By embracing innovation and commitment to sustainable development, humanity can overcome the challenges of population saturation while safeguarding the well-being of current and future generations.

14 THE SATURATION OF THE FASHION AND CLOTHING WORLD

"Trends, Challenges, and Innovations"
In the modern era, the fashion and clothing industry is characterized by saturation, with a proliferation of brands, trends, and consumer choices shaping the global marketplace. This saturation is influenced by a multitude of factors, including globalization, fast fashion, digitalization, and shifting consumer preferences. As stakeholders within the fashion ecosystem navigate this saturated landscape, they encounter both opportunities and challenges in their quest for sustainability, innovation, and market relevance.

Globalization has transformed the fashion industry, enabling the outsourcing of manufacturing to low-cost labour markets and the expansion of supply chains across continents. While this globalization has led to increased accessibility and affordability of clothing for consumers, it has also resulted in supply chain complexity, environmental degradation, and labour exploitation. The saturation of the fashion market is fuelled by the proliferation of fast fashion brands that produce cheap, disposable garments at the expense of ethical and sustainable practices.

The rise of fast fashion has contributed to the

saturation of the clothing world, with brands churning out new collections at an unprecedented pace to meet consumer demand for novelty and trendiness. However, this fast fashion model fosters a culture of disposability, where garments are worn only a few times before being discarded in favor of the next trend. The environmental and social impacts of fast fashion, including textile waste, pollution, and poor working conditions in garment factories, underscore the need for a shift towards more sustainable and ethical practices. Digitalization has revolutionized the fashion industry, providing platforms for brands to connect with consumers, showcase their products, and drive sales through e-commerce, social media, and influencer marketing. Social media influencers wield significant influence over consumer purchasing decisions, driving trends, promoting brands, and shaping perceptions of style and beauty. However, the saturation of digital channels and the commodification of influencer culture raise concerns about authenticity, transparency, and the promotion of unrealistic beauty standards. Amidst the saturation of the fashion world, there is a growing awareness and demand for sustainability and ethical practices within the industry. Consumers are increasingly seeking out brands that prioritize transparency, environmental stewardship, and fair labour practices in their supply chains. This shift towards sustainable fashion encompasses initiatives such as eco-friendly materials, circular design principles, supply chain traceability, and worker empowerment. Moreover, innovative technologies, such as blockchain and digital twins, are being leveraged to improve transparency and accountability throughout the fashion value chain. The saturation of the fashion world has prompted calls for greater diversity, inclusivity, and representation within the industry. Consumers are demanding more diverse and inclusive representation in advertising campaigns, runway shows, and product offerings, challenging traditional beauty standards and promoting body positivity and cultural diversity. Brands that embrace diversity and authenticity stand to resonate with a broader range of consumers and foster a more inclusive and equitable fashion ecosystem. In response to the saturation of fast fashion and disposable culture, there is a growing movement towards slow fashion and conscious consumption. Slow fashion emphasizes quality over quantity, craftsmanship over mass production, and longevity over trendiness. By investing in timeless, well-made garments, consumers can reduce their environmental footprint, support local artisans, and cultivate a more sustainable and mindful approach to fashion consumption.

In grasping the saturation of the fashion and clothing world, stakeholders must prioritize sustainability, innovation, and social responsibility. Brands that embrace transparency, ethical practices, and consumer engagement will be better positioned to thrive in an increasingly competitive marketplace. Moreover, consumers have the power to drive positive change by making informed purchasing decisions, supporting sustainable brands, and advocating for a more inclusive and mindful fashion industry. By embracing innovation and a shared commitment to sustainability, the fashion world can navigate the challenges of saturation while promoting creativity, expression, and social impact.

15 THE SATURATION OF SOCIETY

"Causes and Consequences"

In contemporary society, the phenomenon of saturation has become increasingly prevalent across various aspects of life, from media and technology to consumer goods and cultural trends. This saturation is the result of a combination of societal, economic, and technological factors that have accelerated the pace of change, increased competition, and amplified consumption. Understanding the root causes and consequences of saturation is essential for navigating its complexities and mitigating its adverse effects on individuals and communities.

One of the primary drivers of saturation in society is the rapid pace of technological advancements and digital innovation. The proliferation of smartphones, social media platforms, and digital content creation tools has democratized access to information and entertainment, enabling individuals to produce and consume content at an unprecedented rate. However, this abundance of digital content can lead to information overload, attention fatigue, and a sense of overwhelm as individuals struggle to filter through the vast array of options available to them.

Globalization has transformed the economic

landscape, facilitating the flow of goods, services, and ideas across borders and fuelling market competition. As a result, industries ranging from fashion and food to entertainment and technology have become increasingly saturated with products and brands vying for consumers' attention and loyalty. This saturation can lead to market fragmentation, commodification, and the proliferation of choices, making it challenging for individuals to make informed decisions and find products or services that align with their preferences and values.

As we have explored in the previous chapters, the rise of consumer culture and materialism has contributed to the saturation of society by promoting a relentless pursuit of novelty, status, and consumption. Advertising, marketing, and media influence shape societal norms and aspirations, encouraging individuals to equate happiness and success with the acquisition of material possessions and experiences. However, this culture of consumption has lead to overconsumption, environmental degradation, and social inequality as resources are depleted and wealth becomes increasingly concentrated among a privileged few.

The advent of social media and the rise of digital influencers have amplified the saturation of society by providing platforms for self-expression, personal branding, and content creation. Social media influencers, bloggers, and vloggers wield significant influence over consumer behaviour, shaping trends, promoting products, and shaping cultural norms and values. However, the saturation of social media with curated content, sponsored posts, and advertisements has distorted reality, fostering comparison culture, and contributing to feelings of inadequacy and discontentment among users. The saturation of society is further exacerbated by information overload and fragmentation, where individuals are bombarded with a constant stream of news, opinions, and entertainment from various sources. The advent of digital media and social networking platforms has democratized access to information, but as mentioned earlier in this book, it has also led to the proliferation of echo chambers, filter bubbles, and misinformation. Navigating through this sea of information can be overwhelming, leading to cognitive overload and a sense of disconnection from reality.

Cultural shifts and changing societal values have also contributed to the saturation of society by promoting individualism, instant gratification, and the pursuit of success at all costs. In an increasingly competitive and fast-paced world, individuals may feel pressure to constantly strive for more, leading to a culture of busyness, burnout, and dissatisfaction. Moreover, the erosion of traditional social structures and community ties has exacerbated feelings of isolation and disconnection, further contributing to the saturation of society. In viewing the saturation of society, it is essential to promote mindfulness, critical thinking, and intentional living. By cultivating awareness of the factors contributing to saturation and their impacts on individuals and communities, individuals can make informed choices and prioritize values such as simplicity, sustainability, and human connection.

16 THE ROOT CAUSES OF SATURATION

The saturation of society can be attributed to several interconnected root causes, which have intensified over time and contributed to the overwhelming abundance of information, goods, and choices in contemporary life. Here I present some key root causes. Technological advancements, particularly in the digital realm, have played a significant role in saturating society. The proliferation of smartphones, social media platforms, and digital content creation tools has democratized access to information and enabled individuals to produce and consume content at an unprecedented rate. While technology has undoubtedly improved connectivity and efficiency, it has also led to information overload, attention fatigue, and a constant stream of notifications that can overwhelm individuals and contribute to the saturation of society.

Globalization has transformed the economic landscape, facilitating the flow of goods, services, and ideas across borders and fuelling market competition. As a result, industries ranging from fashion and entertainment to technology and consumer goods have become increasingly saturated with products and brands vying for consumers' attention and loyalty. The rise of fast fashion, disposable consumer goods, and planned obsolescence has further fuelled consumption and contributed to the saturation of society.

A pervasive consumer culture and emphasis on materialism have also contributed to the saturation of society. Advertising, marketing, and media influence shape societal norms and aspirations, encouraging individuals to equate happiness and success with the acquisition of material possessions and experiences. This culture of consumption promotes a cycle of continuous consumption and disposability, contributing to resource depletion, waste generation, and environmental degradation. The advent of digital media and social networking platforms has amplified the saturation of society by providing platforms for self-expression, personal branding, and content creation. Social media influencers, bloggers, and vloggers wield significant influence over consumer behaviour, shaping trends, promoting products, and shaping cultural norms and values. The saturation of digital media with curated content, sponsored posts, and advertisements has distorted reality, fostered comparison culture, and contributed to feelings of inadequacy and discontentment among users. Economic incentives and profit motives also drive the saturation of society, as businesses and corporations seek to maximize profits and market share through aggressive marketing and product expansion strategies. Planned obsolescence, product differentiation, and brand proliferation are common tactics employed to capture consumer attention and drive sales. While these strategies may boost short-term profits, they are contributing to resource depletion, environmental degradation, and societal saturation in the long run.

Social norms and expectations have also played a role in perpetuating the saturation of society. Peer pressure, social comparison, and the desire for status and recognition have influenced individuals' consumption patterns and lifestyle choices. The pressure to keep up with the latest trends, acquire material possessions, and maintain a certain standard of living has led to overconsumption, debt, and dissatisfaction, contributing to the saturation of society and perpetuating a cycle of consumption-driven growth.

The saturation of society is driven by a complex interplay of technological advancements, globalization, consumer culture, digital media, economic incentives, and social norms. Addressing the root causes of saturation requires systemic changes, shifts in societal values, and collective action to promote more sustainable models of development.

17 THE DAMAGING EFFECTS OF SATURATION

The saturation of society, characterized by an abundance of information, goods, and choices, poses significant challenges and risks for the future of humanity. This saturation is driven by factors described in the previous chapter, such as technological advancements, globalization, consumer culture, and changing societal norms, which have profound implications for individual well-being, social cohesion, and environmental sustainability. Understanding the damaging effects of societal saturation is crucial for addressing its root causes and mitigating its impact on future generations.

The saturation of society can have detrimental effects on mental health, contributing to feelings of overwhelm, anxiety, and depression.

Information overload, social comparison, and constant exposure to curated content on social media can erode self-esteem, foster unrealistic expectations, and exacerbate feelings of inadequacy among individuals. Moreover, the pressure to constantly consume and keep up with the latest trends can lead to stress, burnout, and a sense of disconnection from one's authentic self.

The saturation of society with information and digital content has seemingly eroded critical thinking skills and has fostered passive consumption rather than active engagement with ideas and concepts. In an environment characterized by echo chambers, filter bubbles, and misinformation, individuals may struggle to discern fact from fiction and critically evaluate the validity of sources. This decline in critical thinking poses risks to democratic values, informed decision-making, and the ability of individuals to navigate complex societal challenges effectively. Saturation has also contributed to environmental degradation through overconsumption, resource depletion, and pollution. The proliferation of disposable goods, fast fashion, and single-use plastics has exacerbated waste generation and strained natural resources, leading to habitat destruction, biodiversity loss, and climate change. Moreover, the reliance on fossil fuels for energy and transportation has further accelerated environmental degradation, threatening the sustainability of ecosystems and the well-being of future generations. Societal saturation seems to have exacerbated social inequality and fragmentation by widening disparities in access to resources, opportunities, and quality of life. Consumer culture has promoted materialism and conspicuous consumption, which has perpetuated a cycle of wealth accumulation among a privileged few while leaving marginalized communities behind. Moreover, the saturation of digital media and social networking platforms has contributed to social polarization, tribalism, and the erosion of trust and empathy within society.

The saturation of society with globalized media, consumer products, and cultural trends has led to the homogenization and dilution of cultural identity and diversity. Indigenous cultures, traditional practices, and local languages may have been marginalized or may be erased in Favor of dominant Western norms and values. This loss of cultural identity may not only have diminished the richness and vibrancy of human heritage but possibly also have undermined the resilience and adaptability of communities to navigate challenges and preserve their unique identities. Societal saturation perpetuated unsustainable consumption patterns that placed strain on finite resources and contributed to environmental degradation. The pursuit of endless growth and material wealth, fuelled by advertising, marketing, and consumerism, drove overproduction, overconsumption, and waste generation. This linear model of consumption is incompatible with planetary boundaries and ecological limits, threatening the long-term viability of ecosystems and the well-being of future generations. Addressing the damaging effects of societal saturation requires collective action, systemic change, and a shift towards more sustainable and equitable models of development.

Individuals, communities, governments, and businesses must work together now to promote mindfulness, resilience, and social responsibility in the face of saturation. This includes fostering critical thinking skills, promoting media literacy, and cultivating values such as empathy, compassion, and environmental stewardship. By embracing a culture of sustainability, inclusivity, and well-being, we can navigate the challenges of societal saturation and build a more resilient, equitable, and thriving future.

18 STRATEGIES TO REVERSE OR STOP SATURATION

The saturation of society, characterized by information overload, consumerism, and environmental degradation, poses significant challenges to individual well-being, social cohesion, and planetary health. However, by adopting strategic interventions and systemic changes, we can work towards reversing or stopping the saturation of society and promoting a more sustainable, equitable, and fulfilling way forward for humanity. Encouraging mindful consumption is essential for combating the saturation of society. By promoting awareness of the environmental, social, and personal impacts of consumption choices, individuals can make more conscious decisions about what they buy, use, and discard. This includes prioritizing quality over quantity, supporting ethical and sustainable brands, and embracing practices such as minimalism and zero waste.

Promoting media literacy is crucial for empowering individuals to navigate the saturation of digital content and misinformation. Education initiatives that teach critical thinking skills, source evaluation, and fact-checking techniques can help individuals discern credible information from false or misleading sources. Moreover, promoting diverse perspectives and independent journalism fosters a more informed and resilient society. Building resilient communities is essential for addressing the social and environmental challenges of saturation. By fostering strong social connections, mutual support networks, and community-based initiatives, individuals can mitigate the negative effects of saturation and build collective resilience. This includes initiatives such as community gardens, sharing economies, and neighbourhood cooperatives that promote resource sharing, collaboration, and social cohesion. Promoting sustainable lifestyles is critical for reducing the environmental impact of saturation and fostering a more resilient society. Encouraging behaviours such as walking, cycling, and public transit usage reduces reliance on fossil fuels and alleviates congestion and pollution. Moreover, promoting plant-based diets, energy conservation, and renewable energy adoption reduces carbon emissions and promotes environmental sustainability. Transitioning to circular economy models is essential for reducing waste and promoting resource efficiency in society. By designing products for durability, repairability, and recyclability, businesses can minimize the environmental impact of production and consumption cycles. Moreover, embracing practices such as product sharing, leasing, and remanufacturing promotes the reuse and repurposing of resources, reducing the need for virgin materials and mitigating waste generation. Advocating for policy change is crucial for addressing the systemic drivers of saturation and promoting sustainable development. Governments play a key role in implementing regulations, incentives, and initiatives that support sustainability, equity, and well-being. This includes policies such as carbon pricing, extended producer responsibility, and sustainable procurement standards that promote environmental stewardship and social responsibility across sectors. Fostering a culture of well-being is essential for promoting resilience, balance, and fulfilment in society.

Prioritizing mental health, work-life balance, and community engagement fosters a sense of purpose and connection among individuals. Moreover, promoting values such as empathy, compassion, and social responsibility fosters a culture of caring and cooperation that transcends the pressures of consumerism and competition. Embracing technological innovation responsibly is essential for harnessing the potential of technology to address the challenges of saturation. By promoting ethical design, data privacy, and digital inclusion, we can ensure that technological advancements benefit society as a whole. Moreover, leveraging technology to promote sustainability, equity, and well-being, such as through renewable energy, digital healthcare, and smart city initiatives, can contribute to a more resilient and sustainable future. Reversing or stopping the saturation of society then, requires collective action, systemic change, and a commitment to sustainability and well-being.

19 ENVISIONING A SUSTAINABLE AND THRIVING FUTURE FOR HUMANITY

If we can successfully stop the saturation of society and shift towards more sustainable and equitable models of development, the future for humanity holds great promise. By prioritizing well-being, resilience, and environmental stewardship, we can create a future where individuals, communities, and ecosystems thrive in harmony. Here I hypothesise how the future could unfold.

In a future where saturation is no longer the norm, society embraces sustainable consumption and production practices. Products are designed with durability, repairability, and recyclability in mind, reducing waste and minimizing environmental impact. Circular economy models thrive, promoting resource efficiency and closed-loop systems that regenerate natural capital rather than depleting it. Communities are empowered to build resilience and foster social cohesion in the face of challenges. Strong social networks, mutual support systems, and community-based initiatives enable individuals to weather crises and thrive in times of uncertainty. Collaborative approaches to problem-solving and decision-making promote inclusivity, diversity, and collective well-being.

Efforts to halt saturation led to environmental regeneration and biodiversity conservation on a global scale. Ecosystem restoration projects, reforestation efforts, and marine conservation initiatives help heal the planet's ecosystems and safeguard biodiversity. By prioritizing ecological integrity and planetary health, humanity secures a sustainable future for future generations. Advancements in green technologies and renewable energy sources drive the transition towards a carbon-neutral future. Solar, wind, and hydroelectric power become the primary sources of energy, displacing fossil fuels and reducing greenhouse gas emissions. Innovative solutions such as carbon capture and storage further mitigate the impacts of climate change, paving the way for a more sustainable energy future. In a world free from saturation, equitable access to resources and opportunities becomes a reality for all. Policies and initiatives aimed at reducing inequality, promoting social justice, and addressing systemic barriers ensure that no one is left behind. Access to education, healthcare, clean water, and nutritious food is guaranteed as fundamental human rights, fostering a more equitable and inclusive society. Cultural diversity flourishes in a future where saturation is no longer the norm, celebrating the richness and vibrancy of human heritage. Indigenous knowledge systems, traditional practices, and local customs are respected and preserved, contributing to the cultural tapestry of humanity. Global solidarity and cooperation foster peace, understanding, and collaboration across borders, transcending divisions and promoting shared prosperity for everyone.

Thriving ecosystems and sustainable cities define the future landscape of humanity. Green spaces, parks, and urban forests enhance the quality of life for urban residents, promoting health, well-being, and connection with nature. Sustainable urban planning and design prioritize walkability, public transit, and active transportation, reducing congestion, pollution, and sprawl while fostering vibrant, liveable communities. Ethical leadership and responsible governance play a crucial role in shaping the future trajectory of humanity.

Governments, businesses, and civil society organizations collaborate to address global challenges such as climate change, inequality, and social injustice. Transparent, accountable, and participatory decision-making processes ensure that the needs and aspirations of all stakeholders are heard and valued. The future for humanity holds great promise if we can successfully stop the saturation of society and embrace more sustainable, equitable, and resilient models of development.

20 EPILOGUE

As we reach the conclusion of "Saturation" it is essential to reflect on the journey we have embarked upon and consider the profound implications of our exploration into the psychology of social norms and the saturation of society. Throughout the pages of this book, we have delved into the depths of human behaviour, societal dynamics, and the intricate interplay between psychology and culture, uncovering the complex web of influences that shape our lives and our world. We began by examining the roots and psychology of social norms, unravelling the mechanisms that drive conformity, influence, and change within society. From social identity theory to cognitive dissonance, we explored the psychological processes that underlie our adherence to social norms and expectations, shedding light on the ways in which they shape our beliefs, attitudes, and behaviours.

Building upon this foundation, we delved into the saturation of society, dissecting the effects and root causes of this pervasive phenomenon. From technological advancements and globalization to consumer culture and economic incentives, we traced the myriad factors that have propelled society to its current state of abundance and excess. We confronted the environmental, social, and psychological consequences of saturation, recognizing the urgent need for change in order to safeguard the well-being of individuals, communities, and the planet.

Yet, amidst the challenges we face, there is hope—a beacon of light illuminating the path forward. Throughout this book, we have explored strategies for stopping the saturation of society and envisioning a future where sustainability, equity, and well-being take centre stage. From promoting mindful consumption and fostering resilient communities to advocating for policy reform and embracing technological innovation responsibly, we have charted a course towards a more sustainable and fulfilling future for humanity.

But our journey does not end here. As we close

the final chapter of this book, let us remember that the power to effect change lies within each and every one of us. By challenging the status quo, redefining cultural norms, and advocating for a more sustainable and equitable world, we can shape the course of history and create a brighter future for humanity and our planet Earth. As we bid farewell to "Saturation" let us carry forward the lessons learned, the insights gained, and the spirit of inquiry that has guided us on this transformative journey. May we continue to unravel the tapestry of saturation, weaving a new narrative of sustainability, resilience, and hope for all.

Aeron P. White